I0555039

FUNDAMENTALS OF FLAG & TACKLE FOOTBALL

FOR THE STUDENT ATHLETE

CREATED BY
KINGDOM FITNESS RECREATION

FUNDAMENTALS OF
FLAG & TACKLE FOOTBALL
FOR THE STUDENT ATHLETE

CREATED BY

Kingdom Fitness Recreation
42068 LA-621
Gonzales, LA 70737
http://www.kfrec.com/

PUBLISHING

Printed in the U.S.A.
First Printing
February 2023
ISBN 979-8-218-06368-9

EDITOR

Kristie Gauthreaux
Mask Off Publishing

GRAPHIC DESIGN

Cody Sibley
Mystic Spiral Consulting

COPYRIGHT

© 2023 Kingdom Fitness Recreation.
All Rights Reserved.

This book or any portion thereof may not be reproduced or used in
any manner whatsoever without the express written permission of the
publisher except for the use of brief quotations in a book review.

JUST KEEP DOING IT!
Everyone gets better when they
DON'T GIVE UP!
~ Ted Williams ~

CONTENTS

CONTENTS

NOTES

CHAPTER 1

BASICS OF FOOTBALL

THE PLAYING FIELD

FIELD DIMENSIONS

The main playing area of the football field is 100 yards (300 feet) long and 53 ⅓ yards (160 feet) wide.

END ZONES

1. At each end of the field are the areas called the end zones. This area extends the field another ten yards on both sides. The line between the field and the end zone is called the goal line.

2. In order to score a touchdown, some portion of the ball must cross the goal line while in the possession of an offensive player. Any play that takes place outside the lines of the end zone is considered out of bounds.

YARD LINES

After every five yards, a line crosses the field. Every ten yard line of the field is marked with a yardage number. At the center of the field is the fifty yard line. The closer you get to the end zone, the more the yard line decreases from the fifty yard line in each direction.

HASH MARKS

Hash marks are small lines made every yard on the field. These lines help to spot the ball on the field and give an indication of the distance remaining to achieve a first down.

GOAL POSTS

Located at the ends of each end zone and aligned with the center of the field are the field goal posts. The bottom of the field goal post measures as follows:

GOAL POST

END LINE

END ZONE

GOAL LINE

HASH MARKS

HASH MARKS

SIDELINE

TEAM AREA/COACH BOX

300 Feet = 100 Yards

TEAM AREA/COACH BOX

50

SIDELINE

GOAL POST

END ZONE

GOAL LINE

END LINE

160 Feet = 53 1/3 Yards

image by rcsibley@gmail.com

- ○ **College and NFL:** a height of ten feet above the ground and width of eighteen feet, with posts that are six inches wide;

- ○ **High School:** there is a width of twenty three feet with posts that are four inches wide.

SIDE LINES

Side lines are the areas outside of the lines of play and are considered out of bounds. If any part of the player or ball touches the line or beyond, then they are out of bounds.

GOAL LINES

The goal line is the line between the playing field and the end zone.

END LINES

The end line is the line at the back of the end zone.

FORMAT OF THE GAME

TIME DURING THE GAME

1. Football is a timed sport.
2. The team with the most points when the time runs out wins the game.
3. The game is divided up into four periods, or quarters, with a long "half time" between the second and third quarter.
4. Time is counted while plays are running, and sometimes between plays. For example, time continues after a running play where the player was tackled in bounds, but will stop on an incomplete pass.
5. To keep the game going at a good pace, the offense has a limited amount of time called the play clock between plays.

FOOTBALL PLAYERS

1. Each team has to have eleven players on the field at a time. Teams may substitute players between plays with no restrictions.
2. **DEFENSE PLAYERS**
   a. Defensive players may take any position on the field they want and can move about their side of the football prior to the play without restriction.
   b. There are no certain defensive positions, therefore, there are no specific rules defining defensive positions or roles.
3. **OFFENSE PLAYERS**
   a. The offensive players, however, have several rules that define their positions and what roles they may take in the offense.

b. Seven offensive players must be lined up on the line of scrimmage.

c. The other four players must be lined up at least one yard behind the line of scrimmage.

d. All of the offensive football players must be set, or not moving, prior to the play beginning with the exception of one of the four backs, which may be moving parallel or away from the line of scrimmage.

🔑 KEYS OF UNDERSTANDING

Following are the Keys of Understanding that you have learned in this chapter.

✪ The main playing area of the field is 100 yards (300 feet) long by 53 ⅓ yards (160 feet) wide.

✪ At each end of the field is an end zone. This area extends the field another ten yards on each side.

✪ In order to score a touchdown, some portion of the ball must cross the goal line while in the possession of an offensive player.

✪ At the center of the field is the fifty yard line. The closer you get to the end zone, the more the yard line decreases from the fifty yard line in each direction.

✪ At the end of the end zone and centered on the field is the field goal.

✪ Side lines are considered out of bounds.

✪ The goal line is the line between the playing field and the end zone.

✪ The end line is the line located at the back of the end zone.

- ✪ Football is a timed sport. The team with the most points at the end of the time period, wins the game. The game is divided up into four periods or quarters with a long "half time" between the second and third quarter.

- ✪ Each team has to have eleven players on the field at a time.

- ✪ Seven offensive players must be lined up on the line of scrimmage. The other four players must be lined up at least one yard behind the line of scrimmage.

NOTES

CHAPTER 2

PLAYING FOOTBALL

BASIC GAME PLAY

POSSESSION

1. The team with possession of the football is called the **OFFENSE**. The offense tries to advance the football as far as possible towards the opponents' end zone on plays.

2. The team that does not have possession is called the **DEFENSE**. The defense tries to prevent the offense from advancing the football or scoring.

LINE OF SCRIMMAGE

The line of scrimmage is an imaginary line across the width of the field that marks where the ball is placed at the beginning of each play. The OFFENSE and DEFENSE line up on opposite sides of this line.

THE DOWN SYSTEM

1. The offense must advance the ball at least ten yards every four plays, or downs.

2. Each time the offense is successful in advancing the ball ten yards, they receive four more downs, or what is called a first down.

3. If the offense does not advance the ball forward ten yards or more in four plays, the other team gains possession of the football at the current line of scrimmage.

4. In order to prevent the other team from getting good field position the offense can intentionally punt, or kick, the ball to the other team. This is often done on fourth down when the offense is outside of field goal range.

5. Each down is called by its name or number: First, second, third, and fourth down.

EACH PLAY

1. Offensive plays on downs start with what is called a **SNAP**. The snap is when the center passes the football between their legs to one of the offensive backs, in most cases, the quarterback.

2. The play is advanced either by running down the field with the football or throwing the football to one of the other offensive players.

3. The football play is over when:

   a. The player with the football is tackled or goes out of bounds,

   b. An incomplete pass is thrown, or

   c. Someone scores by making a touchdown or a field goal.

LOSING POSSESSION

The offensive team can lose possession of the football by any of the following:

1. Scoring.

2. Not getting ten yards in four downs.

3. Fumbling or dropping the football and the defensive team recovers it.

4. Throwing the football to a defensive player. which is called an interception.

5. Punting or kicking the football to the defensive team.

6. Missing a field goal or getting tackled in the end zone for a safety.

 WAYS TO SCORE

Touchdown	Extra Point
6 Points	1 Point

2 Point Conversion	Field Goal
2 Points	3 Points

Safety
2 Points

TOUCHDOWN - 6 POINTS

1. Scoring touchdowns is the primary goal in football, and they are the method to score the most points at one time in the game.

2. Players score a touchdown when they advance the ball across the other team's goal line into the end zone.

3. Players must have possession of the football and it must "break the plane" of the goal line in order for a touchdown to be scored..

4. After scoring a touchdown, the offensive football team is also awarded the chance for an *Extra Point* or a *2 Point Conversion*.

EXTRA POINT - 1 POINT

1. An extra point can be attempted after a touchdown where the offensive team does a play where they attempt to kick the ball through the field goal posts, or uprights.

2. If the ball goes between the two uprights, the extra point is successful and the team receives one point.
3. If the ball bounces off the uprights without passing between them or passes by the uprights on the outside, either the right side or left side, the extra point attempt is a failure.
4. The attempt to kick the extra point after a touchdown is sometimes called a P.A.T. (Point After Touchdown).

2 POINT CONVERSION - 2 POINTS

1. A two point conversion can be attempted after a touchdown.
2. This play involves the offense making an attempt to get the ball back into the opposing team's end zone again.
3. There are no downs given, and they only have one chance to get the ball across the plane of the goal line, unless a penalty is called on the defense.

FIELD GOAL - 3 POINTS

1. A field goal is when the place kicker on the offensive team kicks the ball through the uprights.
2. A field goal can be attempted at any time, but is usually attempted on fourth down.
3. A field goal is kicked from the yard line on the field where the last down occurred.

SAFETY - 2 POINTS

1. There are several situations in which a safety can be awarded to a team.
2. A safety occurs when the defense tackles an offensive player behind their team's own goal line while the offensive player is in possession of the football.

3. A safety may also be awarded if a defensive player pushes and offensive player out of the end zone while the offensive player is in possession of the football.

4. Once an offensive players is in possession of the football in their own end zone, they must get the *entire football out of the end zone* in order for the defense to not be awarded a safety.

5. A safety is also awarded if a dropped or blocked punt goes through the kicking team's end zone.

6. Sometimes a safety is awarded in the case of a penalty on the offensive football team in the end zone such as holding.

7. After a safety occurs, the defense is awarded 2 points and given possession of the ball by kicking it back to the defense.

 **TIME DURING THE GAME**

HOW LONG IS A FOOTBALL GAME

Football games are divided up into either two halves or four quarters.

MIDDLE SCHOOL	HIGH SCHOOL
4 Quarters	**4 Quarters**
8-10 minutes each	**12 minutes each**

NCAA (COLLEGE)	NFL
4 Quarters	**4 Quarters**
15 minutes each	**15 minutes each**

WHEN DOES THE CLOCK STOP RUNNING?

The game clock will stop in the following situations:

- ✪ During timeouts
- ✪ At the end of each quarter or half
- ✪ When a ball carrier runs out of bounds
- ✪ When a penalty is called
- ✪ When a player is injured
- ✪ When a team scores
- ✪ When the ball changes possession
- ✪ After a play ending in an incomplete pass
- ✪ When the officials need to measure for a first down

✪ When a team gets a first down (high school only)

✪ At the *two minute warning* (NFL only) which is like a time out when there is only two minutes left on the game clock, one before half time and one before the end of the game.

WHAT ARE THE PLAY CLOCKS?

1. There are two different play clocks in football – a **40-Second** play clock and a **25-Second** play clock.

2. 40-Secon Play Clock: The offensive team only has so long to hike the football and start another play. In the case where play is continuing, they have forty seconds from the end of the previous play to start a new play.

3. **25-Second Play Clock:** If play has stopped, like for a timeout, then they have twenty five seconds from the time the referee sets the ball and starts the play clock.

🔑 KEYS OF UNDERSTANDING

Following are the Keys of Understanding that you have learned in this chapter.

✪ The team with possession of the football is called the offense.

✪ The defense tries to prevent the offense from scoring or advancing the football down the field.

✪ The offense must advance the ball at least ten yards every four plays or downs. Each time the offense is successful in advancing the ball ten yards or more, they receive four more downs, or what is called a first down.

✪ The snap is when the center passes the football between their legs to one of the offensive backs, usually the quarterback. The ball is advanced either by running with the football or passing the football.

✪ Know when the football play is over (see topic above).

✪ Know how the offensive team loses possession of the football (see topic above).

✪ Know ways to score along with how many points each is worth (see Way to Score topic above).

✪ Touchdowns are the primary goal in football and they are also worth the most points. Players score a touchdown when they advance the ball across the other team's goal line into the end zone.

✪ An extra point can be attempted after a touchdown where the team kicks the ball through the uprights. This is worth one point and is sometimes called a PAT (Point After Touchdown).

✪ A two point conversion can also be attempted after a touchdown.

✪ A field goal is when the place kicker kicks the ball through the uprights.

✪ A safety occurs when the defense tackles an offensive player behind their team's own goal line.

✪ Know How long is a football game? From above

✪ Know When does the clock stop in football? From above

✪ In the case where play is continuing, the team has forty seconds from the end of the previous play to start a new play. If play has stopped, like for a timeout, then they have twenty-five seconds from the time the referee sets the ball and starts the play clock.

✪ Each down is called by its name or number: First, second, third, and fourth down.

NOTES

CHAPTER 3

FOOTBALL PENALTIES

WHAT ARE PENALTIES?

1. There are many rules and penalties that are enforced during a football game. Penalties occur when one of the rules is broken by a player.

2. Most football penalties result in a loss or gain of yardage, depending on whether the penalty is against the offense or the defense.

3. The severity of the rule infraction determines the the severity of the penalty, such as the number of yards that are gained or lost.

4. Most penalties are five or ten yards, but some personal foul penalties result in fifteen yards. Also, pass interference can result in a penalty that matches the length of the intended pass. This rule varies by the different levels of football.

5. The team that did not commit the penalty has the right to decline the penalty.

6. Football penalties are charged against either the DEFENSE or the OFFENSE.

Penalties Can Result In Any One or More of the Following

5 Yards

10 Yards

Automatic First Down

Loss of a Down

Relay Previous Down

LIST OF PENALTIES

FALSE START	
OFFENSE	DEFENSE
5 YARDS	N/A

A false start is called when a football player on the offense moves just prior to the snap. *Note that only one back on the offense can legally be "in motion" at the time of the snap.*

OFFSIDE	
OFFENSE	DEFENSE
5 YARDS	5 YARDS

An offside penalty is when a player from the offense or defense is on the wrong side of the line of scrimmage at the time of the snap.	When an offensive player does this, it is called "false start". A defensive player can cross the line of scrimmage as long as they get back before the snap, but if they touch an offensive player, they can be called for "encroachment".

HOLDING	
OFFENSE	DEFENSE
10 YARDS	5 YARDS + AUTOMATIC FIRST DOWN

When a player grabs another football player without the ball with their hands, hooks the player, or tackles them.

PASS INTERFERENCE	
OFFENSE	DEFENSE
10 YARDS	**SPOT OF FOUL**
Pass interference can also be called on the offense if the defender has position and is trying to catch the ball.	When a defender contacts a pass receiver after the ball is in the air to prevent him from catching the ball. This call is enforced on the spot of the foul committed by the defense. It is up to the referee to determine. If the contact is before the ball is in the air, it will be called defensive holding.

FACEMASK	
OFFENSE	DEFENSE
15 YARDS	**15 YARDS**
You are not allowed to twist or pull on another player's face mask. This penalty is usually called when the face mask is grabbed during a tackle.	

ROUGHING THE PASSER OR KICKER	
OFFENSE	DEFENSE
N/A	**15 YARDS + AUTOMATIC FIRST DOWN**
To protect quarterbacks and kickers, who are very vulnerable when they are passing or kicking the ball, defensive players are not allowed to run into them after the ball has been thrown or kicked.	

INTENTIONAL GROUNDING

OFFENSE	DEFENSE
10 YARDS OR SPOT OF FOUL + LOSS OF DOWN	**N/A**

When the passer throws the ball nowhere near an eligible receiver or not being outside of where tackles line up off the line of scrimmage.

INELIGIBLE RECEIVER DOWNFIELD

OFFENSE	DEFENSE
5 YARDS	**N/A**

When one of the offensive players who is not an eligible receiver is more than five yards down field from the line of scrimmage during a forward pass.

NEUTRAL ZONE INFRACTION

OFFENSE	DEFENSE
N/A	**5 YARDS**

A neutral zone infraction is when a defensive player crosses the line of scrimmage prior to the snap and then causes an offensive player to move. Rather than call a false start on the offense, the penalty is called on the defensive player.

ILLEGAL FORMATION

OFFENSE	DEFENSE
5 YARDS	**N/A**

The offense must have seven players lined up on the line of scrimmage. Players who are not on the line of scrimmage must be at least one yard back

ILLEGAL MOTION

OFFENSE	DEFENSE
5 YARDS	**N/A**

Only players in the backfield can go into motion. Once in motion, they must either only move parallel to the line of scrimmage or be set prior to the snap. They cannot move towards the line of scrimmage when the ball is snapped.

TOO MANY MEN IN MOTION

OFFENSE	DEFENSE
5 YARDS	**N/A**

Two players cannot be in motion at the same time.

DELAY OF GAME

OFFENSE	DEFENSE
5 YARDS	**N/A**

When the offensive team does not snap the ball before the play clock has expired, they will be given a delay of game penalty.

ILLEGAL SUBSTITUTION

OFFENSE	DEFENSE
5 YARDS	**5 YARDS**

This is typically called when the offensive team breaks the huddle with twelve players. Even if one of them is running off the field, you cannot break the huddle with twelve players.

CHAPTER 3 FOOTBALL PENALTIES

TOO MANY PLAYERS ON THE FIELD	
OFFENSE	DEFENSE
5 YARDS	5 YARDS

Each team may only have eleven players on the field when the ball is snapped. This penalty results in an automatic first down for the offense when the defense has too many players on the field.

ILLEGAL CONTACT	
OFFENSE	DEFENSE
N/A	5 YARDS

Once a receiver is five yards beyond the line of scrimmage, the defensive player may not block or "chuck" him to disrupt his route. Once within the five yards, the defender may block the receiver, but not hold him.

RUNNING INTO THE KICKER	
OFFENSE	DEFENSE
5 YARDS	5 YARDS

This is a penalty that is called to protect the kicker from getting injured while kicking. Depending on the severity of the hit, the referee may also call roughing the kicker, which is a fifteen yard penalty. *Note that if the defender touches or blocks the ball, then the penalty is not called.* Also, if the player is blocked into the kicker by an offensive player, then the penalty should not be called.

TRIPPING	
OFFENSE	DEFENSE
10 YARDS	10 YARDS

Players are not allowed to stick out their leg intentionally in order to trip another player.

SPARING WITH THE HELMET

OFFENSE	DEFENSE
15 YARDS	15 YARDS

Players are not allowed to hit another with the top of their helmet. This especially applies to a quarterback throwing a pass, a receiver while catching a ball, a player on the ground, or a player who is already being tackled.

FAIR CATCH INTERFERENCE

OFFENSE	DEFENSE
N/A	15 YARDS

Once a player calls for a fair catch on a punt return, the defenders may not touch him or the ball unless the ball touches the ground.

CLIPPING BELOW THE WAIST

OFFENSE	DEFENSE
15 YARDS	15 YARDS

This occurs when a player blocks below the waist from behind. This can cause injury when the player "rolls up" onto the players legs.

CHOP BLOCK

OFFENSE	DEFENSE
15 YARDS	N/A

One player is not allowed to block the defender below the thigh at the same time that another player is blocking the defender up high

ILLEGAL CRACKBACK BLOCK	
OFFENSE	DEFENSE
15 YARDS	XXX

One player is not allowed to block the defender below the thigh at the same time that another player is blocking the defender up high

UNNECESSARY ROUGHNESS	
OFFENSE	DEFENSE
15 YARDS	15 YARDS

Anytime that the referee feels that one player is trying to injure another, he may make this call. This includes tackling a player that is out of bounds or hitting a player who is already down.

UNSPORTSMANLIKE CONDUCT	
OFFENSE	DEFENSE
15 YARDS	15 YARDS

This includes acts that are considered by the referee to be unsportsmanlike. It could include bad language, threatening gestures, arguing with the officials, or fighting.

🔑 KEYS OF UNDERSTANDING

Following are the Keys of Understanding that you have learned in this chapter.

Know the penalties by the definition in which they are called and why they are called. Also, understand the yardage given or taken of the penalty if committed.

NOTES

CHAPTER 4

POSITIONS & RESPONSIBILITIES

11 VS 11 TACKLE FOOTBALL

 OFFENSIVE BACKFIELD

OFFENSE

OFFENSIVE LINE

WIDE RECEIVER (WR)

LINE OF SCRIMMAGE

(TE) TIGHT END

(LT) LEFT TACKLE

RUNNING BACK

(RB) (LG) LEFT GUARD

 QUARTER BACK

(QB) (C) CENTER

(RB) (RG) RIGHT GUARD

RUNNING BACK (RT) RIGHT TACKLE

LINE OF SCRIMMAGE

(WR) WIDE RECEIVER

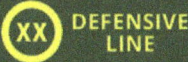

11 vs 11 TACKLE FOOTBALL

XX DEFENSIVE LINE   # DEFENSE   DEFENSIVE BACKFIELD **XX**

CORNERBACK **CB**

LINE OF SCRIMMAGE

FREE SAFETY **FS**

OUTSIDE LINE BACKER **LB**

RIGHT DEFENSIVE END **DE**

DEFENSIVE TACKLE 2 **DT**

MIDDLE LINE BACKER **LB**

DEFENSIVE TACKLE 1 **DT**

LB

LEFT DEFENSIVE END **DE**

OUTSIDE LINE BACKER

SS STRONG SAFETY

LINE OF SCRIMMAGE

CORNERBACK **CB**

Image by ccsibley@gmail.com

11 VS 11 FOOTBALL POSITIONS

OFFENSIVE LINE: The OFFENSE lines up behind the *line of scrimmage* **WITH POSSESSION** of the football. The Offensive Line, sometimes called the Interior Line, is mainly responsible for blocking the defense of the other team. Their primary goal is to protect the quarterback. Offensive linemen do not handle the ball, other than the snap from the center, unless the ball is fumbled. The following positions are part of the Offensive Line.

CENTER (C): The Center begins play from the *Line of Scrimmage* by snapping the ball to the *Quarterback* or another player. *Note: When the ball is snapped to a player other than the quarterback, such as a running back, it is called a Direct Snap.*

OFFENSIVE GUARD (OG/LG/RG): The Offensive Guard is two guards that line up on the left side (*Left Guard* - LG) and right side (*Right Guard* - RG) of the *Center*. Their job is to block and protect the *Quarterback*.

On some plays, a Guard will push forward to block and open space for a ball carrier to push through the *Defensive Line*. This is most common in *Trap* plays (inside runs), *Sweep* plays (outside runs), and *Screen* plays (short passes). When used in this capacity, the guard is called a *Pulling Guard*.

OFFENSIVE TACKLE (OT/LT/RT): The Offensive Tackle is two tackles that line up on the left side (*Left Tackle*) and the right side (*Right Tackle*) of the two *Offensive Guards*. Their job is to block and protect the *Quarterback*. They specifically protect the *Quarterback* from getting hit from behind, known as the *blind side*.

OFFENSIVE BACKFIELD: The Offensive Backfield mostly consists of *backs* and *receivers*. The roles of each of the *Backfield* players vary depending on what the play call is. The following positions are part of the Offensive Backfield.

QUARTERBACK (QB): The Quarterback receives the ball from the **Center** when the ball is *snapped*. This action starts the play. The **Quarterback**'s responsibility is to receive the play from the coaches on the sideline, communicate the play to the other *Offensive Players* in a *huddle*, and implement the play after the *snap* in order to move the ball further down the field past the *line of scrimmage*.

The Quarterback usually lines up in one of three positions at the start of the play:

✪ **Under Center:** The **QB** lines up directly behind and in contact with the **Center** and receives the ball by direct hand-to-hand pass at the *snap*.

✪ **Pistol Formation:** The **QB** lines up directly, but some distance behind the **Center** and receives the ball by a *snap pass* from the **Center**. A *snap pass* is a backward pass made from the line of scrimmage between the legs of the *Center*.

✪ **Shotgun Formation:** The **QB** lines up directly behind the *Center* like in the **Pistol Formation** but is further away from the *Center* and receives the ball by a *snap pass* from the Center as described above.

Once the snap occurs and the play has started, the QB has three options for how to move the ball down the field past the line of scrimmage.

- ✪ **Scramble:** The *QB* can keep the ball and run it forward to progress the ball further down the field.

- ✪ **Hand-Off:** The *QB* can hand the ball off to another eligible ball carrier so they can run it (or occasionally *Forward Pass* it) to progress the ball further down the field..

- ✪ **Forward Pass:** The *QB* can throw the ball forward to an eligible receiver who can progress the ball further down the field.

RUNNING BACKS (HB/FB): Running Backs line up behind the ***Offensive Line*** in positions that make them able to receive the football by a *hand-off* from the *QB*. It is common for there to be zero to three running backs in a play. If there are no running backs, it is referred to as having an ***Empty Backfield***. Following are the different types of *Running Backs*:

- ✪ **Halfback (HB):** The Half Back, also called the *Tailback* is usually the primary ball carrier on a *rushing* (or running) play. They may also catch a pass, usually when the ***Wide Receivers*** are covered by ***Defensive Players***. Halfbacks usually line of to one or both sides of the *QB* and often a little behind the *QB*.

- ✪ **Fullback (FB):** The Fullback is often larger and stronger than the *HB*. They are often used as blockers but also can *rush* or *catch a pass*. ***Fullbacks*** often line up closer to the *line of scrimmage* than other ***Halfbacks***.

WIDE RECEIVER (WR):   Wide Receivers are the players who catch the ball when it is thrown, or passed, by another member of the *Offense*, usually the *QB*. Wide receivers often line up in the *Backfield* *split-wide* near the sidelines. Their main goal is to run pass routes and get "open" which is to find a way to get clear of a defender so they can catch a pass. There are a few types of *Wide Receivers*.

- ✪ **Split End:** Lines up on the *line of scrimmage*.

- ✪ **Flanker:**   Lines up behind the *line of scrimmage* with the backs.

- ✪ **Slot Receiver:** Lines up between the outer most *Wide Receiver* and the *Offensive Line*. This Receiver is said to be "*in the slot*".

- ✪ **Wide Back:**   This *Wide Receiver* is also capable of playing the role of a *Running Back*.

TIGHT END (TE):   Tight ends line up on either side of the Offensive Line and directly next to the Defensive Tackles. A Tight End may also line up behind the line of scrimmage and be considered a back. The *Tight End* is a cross between a *Wide Receiver* and an *Offensive Lineman*. Their role depends on where they line up at the start of the play and what play is called by the coaches.

DEFENSIVE LINE: The **DEFENSE** team begins play at the *line of scrimmage* **WITHOUT POSSESSION** of the football. The *Defensive Line* lines up directly on the *line of scrimmage* across from the *Offensive Line*. The following two positions are considered part of the *Defensive Line*.

DEFENSIVE TACKLE (DT): The Defensive Tackle, sometimes called a *Defensive Guard* plays at the center of the *Defensive Line* and lines up at the *line of scrimmage*. Their responsibility is to stop the *Offense* from making running plays through the center of the *line of scrimmage*. If a *Defensive Tackle* lines up directly across from the *Center* of the *Offensive Line*, that Tackle is called the *Nose Tackle* or *Nose Guard*. There are usually one or two *Defensive Tackles* on the line.

DEFENSIVE END (DE): Just outside the *Defensive Tackles* at the *line of scrimmage* are the *Defensive Ends* also called *Defensive Guards*. Their responsibility is to stop the **OFFENSE** from making plays on the outside edges. *Defensive Linemen* often take a stance with one or both hands on the ground prior to the *snap*. These positions are known as a *Three-Point-Stance* and a *Four-Point-Stance*. This helps tell the difference between a *Lineman* and a *Linebacker*.

DEFENSIVE BACKFIELD: The *Defensive Backfield* is where you find *Linebackers* and *Defensive Backs*.

LINEBACKERS (OLB/MLB): *Linebackers* line up behind the *Defensive Line* and have different responsibilities depending on the play. They have three primary *DEFENSIVE RESPONSIBILITIES*:
1. Rush the passer,
2. Defend against the run, or
3. Cover receivers in a pass play.

    ✪ **Outside Linebackers:** There are three main types of Outside Linebacker.

        ★ *Outside Linebacker (OLB):* All *OLB* line up on the same side of the *Defensive Line*.

★ *Strongside Linebacker (SLB):* The *SLB* lines up directly across from a *Tight End* and is responsible for covering the *Tight End* or *Running Back* on pass plays.

★ *Weakside Linebacker (WLB):* The *WLB* lines up on the side of the field that does not have a *Tight End*. The *WLB* is often used to *rush* or *blitz* the **Quarterback** or to cover a **Running Back** on a pass play.

○ **Middle Line Backer (MLB):** The *Middle Linebacker* sometimes called the *Inside Linebacker* are an important part of the **DEFENSE**. They are used for all three *defensive responsibilities* listed above.

DEFENSIVE BACKS (DB/CB/S): The *Defensive Backs* are also known as the "*secondary*" line up in the *Backfield* either behind the *linebackers* or outside near the *side lines*. Their primary job is to defend against pass plays made by the **OFFENSE** and act as the backup plan for defending running plays. Following are the types of *Defensive Backs* usually found in the *Defensive Backfield*.

○ **Cornerback (C):** The job of the *CB* is to disrupt pass plays by preventing the **Receiver** from catching the pass by swatting it away or by catching the pass (an *interception*). In a running play, the *CB* is to assist the rest of the **DEFENSE** in stopping the runner.

○ **Safety (S):** The *Safety* is the furthest **DEFENSE** player from the *line of scrimmage* and usually helps the *CB* with preventing the successful deep pass. There are two types of *Safety* positions.

+ ***Strong Safety (SS):*** The *Strong Safety* provides extra protection against a run play and usually stands closer to the *line of scrimmage* opposite the **Tight End**.

+ ***Free Safety (FS):*** The **Free Safety** is usually the furthest from the *line of scrimmage* and primarily protects against a long pass play.

○ **Other Backs:** Some DEFENSE plays take one of the Linemen or a Linebacker to gain extra pass coverage.

+ ***Nickelback:*** When there are 5 *Defensive Backs*, the play is called a *Nickel Package* and the 5th back is the **Nickelback**.

+ ***Dimeback:*** When there are 6 *Defensive Backs*, the play is called a *Dime Package (2 Nickelbacks)* and the 6th back is the **Dimeback**.

SPECIAL TEAMS: *Special Teams* are the members of the teams that are on the field during kick plays. Some *Special Teams* roles are the same as the roles on **OFFENSE** or **DEFENSE**. For example, *Offensive Linemen* block and protect the **Kicker** while *Defensive Players* tackle and disrupt. Some *Special Teams* roles, however, are unique to the **Kick** play. Most *Special Teams* players, other than the **Kicker** and **Punter** also play skill positions on **OFFENSE** or **DEFENSE**.

KICKER (K): The *Kicker*, also called the *Placekicker*, kick the football during *kickoffs*, *extra points*, and *field goals*. They kick the ball from either the hands of the **Holder (H)** or off a *tee*.

PUNTER (P): The *Punter* usually lines up 15 yards behind the *line of scrimmage*. When the **Punter** gets the ball after the *snap*, usually on 4th down, they drop the ball and kick it to the other team.

HOLDER (H):   The *Holder* usually lines up 7 - 8 yards behind the *line of scrimmage* and holds the ball for the **Kicker**. A *Holder* is occasionally used for a *Kickoff* if field conditions make using a tee impossible. This position is often filled by a backup *Quarterback*.

LONG SNAPPER (LS):   *The Long Snapper* is a **Center** who *snaps* the ball to the ball **Holder** who holds the ball for the **Kicker**. This position is different from the **Center** because the ball has to *snapped* much further back than on regular **OFFENSE** plays.

RETURNER: The Kick Returner is the one who catches a kicked ball and runs it back across the field. There are two types of Returners:

⚙ **Kick Returner (KR):**   Catches and returns the football on a *Kickoff* play.

⚙ **Punt Returner (PR):**   Catches and returns the football on a *Punt* play.

5 vs 5 FLAG FOOTBALL
⊗ OFFENSE AND DEFENSE ⊗

LINE OF SCRIMMAGE

WIDE RECEIVER WR

DB DEFENSIVE BACK

SAFETY S

CENTER

QUARTER BACK QB C

R RUSHER

SAFETY S

WIDE RECEIVER WR

DB DEFENSIVE BACK

WIDE RECEIVER WR

LINE OF SCRIMMAGE

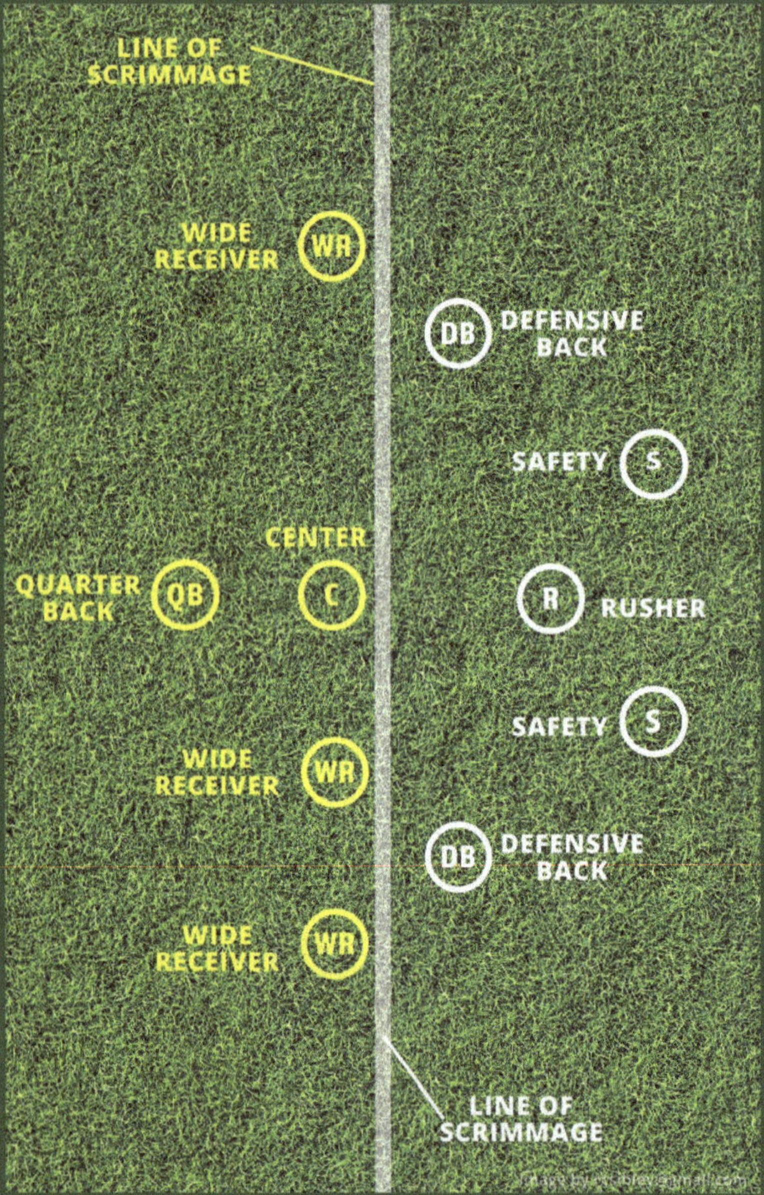

5 VS 5 FLAG FOOTBALL POSITIONS

UNIQUE EQUIPMENT: In **Flag Football**, players wear belts with *flags* that hang along their sides. Each team has a different color flag. Instead of physically tackling other players, **Flag Football** players pull the flags from their opponents' belts. Players receive flags and belts from their coaches or league organizers.

OFFENSE: The **OFFENSE** lines up behind the *line of scrimmage* **WITH POSSESSION** of the football. Following are the four most common **OFFENSE** positions in *Flag Football*.

QUARTERBACK (QB): The *Quarterback* lines up directly behind the *Center*. The *QB* receives the *snap* from the *Center* and passes the ball or hands it off to a runner. The *QB* has seven seconds to pass or handoff the ball. If they do not, the play is dead.

The QB is not allowed to run with the ball after the snap unless the ball is handed off to a teammate then handed back to them.

The QB has other responsibilities as well such as being able to scan the field to find open *Wide Receivers*, have awareness of the **DEFENSE**, be able to *scramble* to avoid a defensive pass rush, and perhaps most importantly be a leader and be able to think and perform under pressure.

CENTER (C): The *Center* lines up directly on the *line of scrimmage*. The main job of the *Center* is to snap the ball to the *QB* to start the play. Once the ball has been *snapped* to the *QB*, the *Center* can act as a *Wide Receiver* and run across the *line of scrimmage* to be a potential target for a *pass play*.

WIDE RECEIVER (WR): The *Running Back* usually lines up either on the line of scrimmage or back from the line of scrimmage to one or both sides of the *Center* and the *Quarterback*. Teams usually have two or three *Wide Receivers* on the field a the same time.

Any **OFFENSE** player who does not receive the ball after the *snap* is eligible to catch a *pass play* as a *Wide Receiver* once the *QB* has the ball and the play has started. *Wide Receivers* run specific routes based on what play is called by the coaches. In addition to catching pass plays, all *WR* players are also able to take a *handoff* of the ball from the *QB* and function as a *Running Back*.

RUNNING BACK (RB): The *Running Back* usually lines up in the *Backfield* then moves forward after the snap so they can be a potential target for a *handoff* from the *QB*.. Depending on the play, there can be zero to three *Running Backs* on the field and they line up on one or both sides of the *Center* and the *Quarterback*. The main job of a *Running Back* is to take a *handoff* from the *Quarterback* after the *snap* then run the ball across the *line of scrimmage*.

A *Running Back* is also eligible to *throw a pass* to another player or to act as a *Wide Receiver* and be the target of a *pass play*.

DEFENSE: The **DEFENSE** lines up on the opposite side of *line of scrimmage* from the **OFFENSE WITHOUT POSSESSION** of the football. Following are the four most common **DEFENSE** positions in *Flag Football*.

DEFENSIVE BACK (DB):   The *Defensive Backs* usually line up a few yards back from the *line of scrimmage* on either side of the **Center.**   Their primary job is to cover the *Wide Receivers* and defend against the *pass play* by swatting the ball away of catching the pass for an *interception*. They may also pull the flag from the belt of a running ball carrier. A *DB* must be able to quickly detect if the **OFFENSE** is running a *pass play* or a *running play* and adapt their reaction appropriately.

SAFETY (S):   The *Safety* lines up further back from line of scrimmage. Their main job to stop opponents who break through the rest of the **DEFENSE**. They track the ball. If it is a run, they prepare to stop the runner if they get past the rest of the **DEFENSE**. If it is a pass play they cover the *Wide Receiver*. The ultimate goal is to prevent the **OFFENSE** from scoring points.

RUSHER (R):   The *Rusher* lines up a minimum of 7 yards from the *line of scrimmage*. If the paying field does not have yard lines, officials will mark this seven yard zone before every play. The main job of the *Rusher* is to prevent the *Quarterback* from passing the ball after the snap. This is called *rushing the passer*.

🔑 KEYS OF UNDERSTANDING

Following are the Keys of Understanding that you have learned in this chapter.

> ✪ Know the positions of the offensive and defensive football players, as seen in the pictures underneath the "11 versus 11 Tackle Football".

> ✪ Know the responsibilities of the skill positions on offense and defense, as seen in the picture underneath the "5 versus 5 Flag Football".

NOTES

CHAPTER 5

KF RECREATION ROUTE TREE

KINGDOM FITNESS RECREATION
ROUTE TREE

SIGNAL **# 0**	ROUTE **SPOT**	SIGNAL **Snap Fingers**
SIGNAL **# 1**	ROUTE **HITCH**	SIGNAL **Finger Pointing to Ring Finger on the Opposite Hand**
SIGNAL **# 2**	ROUTE **SLANT**	SIGNAL **Swipe Corner of Eye**
SIGNAL **# 3**	ROUTE **OUT**	SIGNAL **Hands "Closed Fist" with Thumb Pointing Out Away From Hip**
SIGNAL **# 4**	ROUTE **IN**	SIGNAL **Hand "Open Hand" Waving in Front of the Body at Pelvis Level**

KINGDOM FITNESS RECREATION
ROUTE TREE

SIGNAL # 5	ROUTE **COME BACK**	SIGNAL **Hand Hitting Back of Shoulder**
SIGNAL # 6	ROUTE **CURL**	SIGNAL **Finger Marking a "Curly Hair" Motion on the Side of the Head**
SIGNAL # 7	ROUTE **CORNER**	SIGNAL **Arm Raised Pointing at Elbow of the Opposite Arm**
SIGNAL # 8	ROUTE **POST**	SIGNAL **Two Hands "Closed Fist" Like Putting a Post in the Ground**
SIGNAL # 9	ROUTE **GO**	SIGNAL **Nod Head Like Saying "Yes"**

NOTES

CHAPTER 6

WEEKLY HOMEWORK: OFFENSE

QUARTERBACK

Proper Stance
☐ × 8 Under Center
☐ × 8 Shotgun/Pistol

Pass the Ball
☐ × 10 from the Knee: *Same knee, as throwing arm, with knee on the ground*
  » CUES:
    Toe, Elbow, Throw

☐ × 10 from Split/Staggered Stance: *Opposite Foot Forward of Throwing Arm.*
  » CUES:
    Toe, Elbow, Throw

☐ × 10 from a 3-Step Drop Back from Under Center
  » CADENCE + *CUES:*
    Toe, Elbow, Throw

☐ × 10 from a 3-Step Drop Back from Pistol/Shotgun
  » CADENCE + *CUES:*
    Toe, Elbow, Throw

VIDEO LINKS
See Pages 54-55

 **WIDE RECEIVER**

Proper Stance
☐ × 8 Outside foot closest to the sideline needs to be back (mainly for all receivers on the field). Hands ready properly.

Proper Takeoff
Proper takeoff when getting off the line of scrimmage.
☐ × 3 from Left Side
☐ × 3 from Right Side

Run Routes
☐ × 2 Each Route

☐ 0 Spot	☐ 5 Comeback
☐ 1 Hitch	☐ 6 Curl
☐ 2 Slant	☐ 7 Corner
☐ 3 Out	☐ 8 Post
☐ 4 In	☐ 9 Go

Catch the Ball
Catch Ball at Different Angles
☐ × 10 Each One

☐ High	☐ Low
☐ Right Side	☐ Left Side
☐ Over Right Shoulder	
☐ Over Left Shoulder	

Look and Catch
☐ × 50 Catch a tennis ball or a football.
» CUE: Look the ball all the way into the catch

VIDEO LINKS
See Pages 54-55

 RUNNING BACK

Stance + Lead Steps
Always start in the proper stance in the **BACKFIELD** and take the proper lead steps.
☐ × 10 Steps to the Right
☐ × 10 Steps to the Left

Handoff Steps
Always start in the proper stance, take the proper lead steps, and identify the hole to run through. Always keep eyes down field while running.
☐ × 2 CHECK SWING
☐ × 2 CHECK DOWN
☐ × 2 CHECK OUT
☐ × 2 CHECK IN
☐ × 2 QUICK OUT
☐ × 2 ANGLE
☐ × 2 WHEEL

Run Routes
☐ × 2 LEAD   ☐ × 2 ZONE
☐ × 2 DIVE   ☐ × 2 PITCH
☐ × 2 SWEEP ☐ × 2 COUNTER

Look and Catch
☐ × 50 Catch a tennis ball or a football.
» CUE: Look the ball all the way into the catch

VIDEO LINKS
See Pages 54-55

SNAPPER/BLOCKER

Snaps + Blocks
- ☐ × 10 Snap Between the Legs
- ☐ × 10 Snap From the Knee
- ☐ × 10 Snap From Standing
- ☐ × 10 Snap From the Knee While Turning
  + Block Straight Back
- ☐ × 10 Snap From the Knee While Turning
  + Block to the Right
- ☐ × 10 Snap From the Knee While Turning
  + Block to the Left
- ☐ × 5 Snap From the Knee While Turning
  + Block Straight Back
  + Check Down
- ☐ × 5 Snap From the Knee While Turning
  + Block Straight Back
  + Check Out
- ☐ × 5 Snap From the Knee While Turning
  + Block Straight Back
  + Check In

Look and Catch
- ☐ × 50 Catch a tennis ball or a football.
  - » CUE: Look the ball all the way into the catch

VIDEO LINKS
See Pages 54-55

VIDEOS FOR QUARTERBACK

- ✪ **https://youtu.be/qtX8WZMWzi0**
  Proper QB stance under center
- ✪ **https://youtu.be/ATrnTJeB78M**
  Proper QB Shotgun/Pistol stance
- ✪ **https://youtu.be/vFi2ln9MA64**
  Proper QB throwing motion
- ✪ **https://youtu.be/M0pr8Zxek4U**
  Drops for the QB

VIDEOS FOR WIDE RECEIVER

- ✪ **https://youtu.be/WY1YoT7z4wl**
  How to receive the football
- ✪ **https://youtu.be/hjyVapPNMkc**
  Proper WR stance for route running
- ✪ **https://youtu.be/AwHpwgZcJkk**
  Proper WR take offs for route running
- ✪ **https://youtu.be/ALZlcJ5ADk8**
  WR route tree

VIDEOS FOR CENTER

- ✪ **https://youtu.be/VWTJ-ew8xrY**
  Snaps from the center
- 2.**https://youtu.be/e6Jh1SzL5Fc**
  Snaps from the center & blocking
- 3. **https://youtu.be/Gl0t8pyswjg**
  Center snaps + Check down
- 4. **https://youtu.be/ynnJTztMj_4**
  Center snaps + check in/out

VIDEOS FOR RUNNING BACK

- https://youtu.be/yhNqzGR7lmo
  RB Depth / Distance
- https://youtu.be/b1cE7QS2YDw
  RB Proper stance and starts
- https://www.youtube.com/shorts/khJl9iqunKs

RB lead from under center

- https://youtu.be/jloGC3NeBag
  RB dive from Shotgun
- https://youtube.com/shorts/ZW0rMYh7pnw
  RB dive from under center
- https://youtu.be/pLee5GBqKaw
  RB stretch from under center
- https://youtu.be/KC5ezx96aF4
  RB counter from under center
- https://youtu.be/sEqZe7JSMIQ
  RB toss from under center
- https://youtu.be/ogWVqjHN2Rw
  RB check swing from shotgun
- https://youtu.be/l1StMWmCypk
  RB passing plays from out the backfield

VIDEOS FOR OFFENSIVE LINEMAN

- https://youtu.be/Aj78XgsNquM
  For the offensive lineman
- https://youtu.be/yHxEZUqEozQ
  Offensive lineman zone or base steps
- https://youtu.be/JTEQh24ddEU
  Offensive lineman pass blocking
- https://youtu.be/FKXdYWSPV6U
  Offensive lineman pulls
- https://youtu.be/LVyHi8vT7eI
  Center snaps for to QB

NOTES

CHAPTER **7**

WEEKLY HOMEWORK: DEFENSE

◀────▶ DEFENSIVE BACK ◀────▶

Back Pedal

- ☐ × 4 Back Pedal, Straight
- ☐ × 2 Each Way; Back Pedal T-Cut or Straight + Comeback Down Hill
- ☐ × 2 Each Way; Back Pedal T-Cut or Straight + 45° Comeback
- ☐ × 2 Back Pedal T-Cut or Straight + Open Up To the Right
- ☐ × 2 Back Pedal T-Cut or Straight + Open Up To the Left
- ☐ × 2 Back Pedal T-Cut or Straight + Open Up To the Right Then Flip Left
- ☐ × 2 Back Pedal T-Cut or Straight + Open Up To the Left Then Flip Right

Blitz

- ☐ × 2 Corner Blitz From Right
- ☐ × 2 Corner Blitz From Left

Look and Catch

- ☐ × 50 Catch a tennis ball or a football.
  - » CUE: Look the ball all the way into the catch

VIDEO LINKS

See Pages 62-63

DEFENSIVE LINE

Rush

- ☐ × 2 Straight Rush
- ☐ × 2 Straight Rush
  Swim Move Right
- ☐ × 2 Straight Rush
  Swim Move Left
- ☐ × 2 Straight Rush
  Rip Move Right
- ☐ × 2 Straight Rush
  Rip Move Left
- ☐ × 2 Rush Right
  Swim Move Left
- ☐ × 2 Rush Left
  Swim Move Right
- ☐ × 2 Rush Right
  Rip Move Left
- ☐ × 2 Rush Left
  Rip Move Right
- ☐ × 2 Straight Rush
  Outside Spin
- ☐ × 2 Straight Rush
  Inside Spin
- ☐ × 2 Rush Right
  Spin Move Left
- ☐ × 2 Rush Left
  Rip Move Right

VIDEO LINKS
See Pages 62-63

 **LINEBACKERS**

Blitz
- ☐ × 2 Blitz Right
- ☐ × 2 Blitz Left

Lateral Shuffle + Run
- ☐ × 2 Lateral Shuffle
  + Run Right
- ☐ × 2 Lateral Shuffle
  + Run Left

Back Pedal
- ☐ × 2 Each Way; Back Pedal
  T-Cut or Straight
  + Comeback Down Hill
- ☐ × 2 Each Way; Back Pedal
  T-Cut or Straight
  + 45° Comeback
- ☐ × 2 Each Way; Back Pedal
  T-Cut or Straight
  + Open Up to the Right
- ☐ × 2 Each Way; Back Pedal
  T-Cut or Straight
  + Open Up to the Left

Look and Catch
- ☐ × 50 Catch a tennis ball or
  a football.
  - » CUE: Look the ball all
    the way into the catch

VIDEO LINKS
See Pages 62-63

 RUSHERS

Blitz
- ☐ × 2 Blitz Right
- ☐ × 2 Blitz Left

Lateral Shuffle + Run
- ☐ × 2 Lateral Shuffle + Run Right
- ☐ × 2 Lateral Shuffle + Run Left

Back Pedal
- ☐ × 2 Each Way; Back Pedal T-Cut or Straight + Comeback Down Hill
- ☐ × 2 Each Way; Back Pedal T-Cut or Straight + 45° Comeback
- ☐ × 2 Each Way; Back Pedal T-Cut or Straight + Open Up to the Right
- ☐ × 2 Each Way; Back Pedal T-Cut or Straight + Open Up to the Left

Look and Catch
- ☐ × 50 Catch a tennis ball or a football.
  - » CUE: Look the ball all the way into the catch

VIDEO LINKS
See Pages 62-63

VIDEOS FOR CORNERBACK

⊗ **https://youtube.com/shorts/8HeOG8MqjVU**
Cornerback Basics

⊗ **https://youtube.com/shorts/JRzpfFNlBLA**
Cornerback backpedal to sprint forward

⊗ **https://youtube.com/shorts/lv63ygRPKsc**
Cornerback backpedal to sprint right/left diagonally

⊗ **https://youtube.com/shorts/WW6686m9CoU**
Backpedal to open up right or left

⊗ **https://youtube.com/shorts/BaiAwzvKL4I**
Backpedal to opening to the right or left + speed turn downhill

⊗ **https://youtu.be/LHaCkIzlEPM**
Backpedal to opening to r/l to a up field diagonal speed turn

⊗ **https://youtube.com/shorts/6Kn4CpEZuXI**
Cornerback Blitz

⊗ **https://youtu.be/7zPkVc00jyM**
Cornerback Drills Live

"I may win and I may lose, but I will never be defeated."
–Emmitt Smith

🏈 VIDEOS FOR LINEBACKER

✪ **https://youtu.be/imlUeYeCz-4**
Linebacker blitz

✪ **https://youtu.be/MlRGBAUFfto**
Linebacker coverages

🏈 VIDEOS FOR DEFENSIVE LINEMAN

✪ **https://youtu.be/xnnc6-er6YM**
Defensive Lineman basics

NOTES

CHAPTER

NUTRITION GUIDE

 DAILY REQUIREMENT

All Players Need the Following Each Day

GRAINS

VEGETABLES

MEAT + BEANS

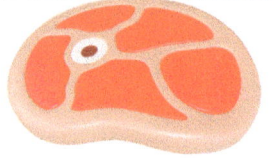

FRUITS

MILK

WATER

 HYDRATION

BEFORE	DURING	AFTER
TRAINING AND/OR COMPETITION	TRAINING AND/OR COMPETITION	TRAINING AND/OR COMPETITION
16 FL OZ	**6-8** FL OZ	**16** FL OZ
	EVERY 15 MINUTES	

RECOMMENDED FOODS

✪ LIQUIDS
- ★ Water
- ★ Sports Drinks
  - + Body Armor
  - + Gatorade
  - + Powerade
  - + Etc.
- ★ Milk

✪ CARBOHYDRATES
- ★ Whole Wheat Bread
- ★ Red Potatoes
- ★ Sweet Potatoes
- ★ Whole Wheat Pasta
- ★ Brown Rice
- ★ Oatmeal
- ★ Cereal
- ★ Tortillas/Wraps

✪ FRUITS
- ★ Apples
- ★ Bananas
- ★ Blueberries
- ★ Grapes
- ★ Strawberries
- ★ Watermelon
- ★ Pineapple
- ★ Oranges
- ★ Peas
- ★ Grapefruit

✪ VEGETABLES
- ★ Spinach
- ★ Avocado
- ★ Broccoli
- ★ Green Beans
- ★ Cauliflower
- ★ Onions
- ★ Collard Greens
- ★ Kale
- ★ Carrots
- ★ Green Peas

✪ PROTEIN
- ★ Kidney Beans
- ★ Seafood
- ★ Lean Beef
- ★ Poultry
- ★ Eggs
- ★ Pork
- ★ Deli Meats

✪ FATS
- ★ Cooking Oil

✪ CONDIMENTS AND TOPPINGS
- ★ Ketchup
- ★ Lettuce
- ★ Margarine
- ★ Tomatoes
- ★ Pickles
- ★ Salsa
- ★ Mustard
- ★ Mayonnaise
- ★ BBQ Sauce
- ★ Italian Dressing

✪ SMART SNACKS
- ★ PB&J
- ★ Granola Bars
- ★ Nuts & Seeds
- ★ Sunchips (All)
- ★ Multigrain Tostitos
- ★ Boom Chicka Pop
- ★ Popcorn
- ★ Multigrain Wheat Thins
- ★ Quaker True Delights
- ★ Multigrain Crisps
- ★ Graham Crackers
- ★ Teddy Grahams

NOTES

INDEX

 INDEX

INDEX

www.ingramcontent.com/pod-product-compliance
Lightning Source LLC
Chambersburg PA
CBHW051331120626
46547CB00016B/2497